CHRISTIANITY

AND THE ENCOUNTER OF THE

WORLD RELIGIONS

NUMBER 14
BAMPTON LECTURES IN AMERICA
DELIVERED AT COLUMBIA UNIVERSITY
1961

PAUL TILLICH

# Christianity

# and the Encounter of the

# World Religions

COLUMBIA   UNIVERSITY   PRESS

New York and London

*To* PROFESSOR YASAKA TAKAGI
*who made my trip*
*to Japan possible*

# PREFACE

THE four Bampton Lectures for 1962 published in this small volume were given in the fall of 1961 in the Low Memorial Library of Columbia University. The printed text is essentially the same as that of the oral delivery. Larger additions would have required more work and more time than was at my disposal, and would have changed the character and original intention of the lectures. They were not supposed to give embracing answers to the manifold problems raised in the discussion of the subject matter, but to confront the reader with some points of view which I consider decisive for every approach to the central problem. Among them are the emphasis on and the characterization of the quasi-religions, the elaboration of the universalist element in Christianity, the suggestion of a dynamic typology of the religions, the dialogical character of the encounter of high religions, and the judgment of Christianity against itself as a religion and its ensuing openness for criticism, both from religions in the proper sense and from quasi-religions.

It is my hope that the presentation of these ideas, in spite of its briefness, will arouse critical thought not only with respect to the relation of Christianity to the world religions but also with respect to its own nature.

PAUL TILLICH

*Harvard University*
*Spring, 1962*

# CONTENTS

# One

## A VIEW OF THE PRESENT SITUATION: RELIGIONS, QUASI-RELIGIONS, AND THEIR ENCOUNTERS

I wish to express my thanks for the honor of having been invited to give the fourteenth lectureship in this important series at the university where, more than twenty-seven years ago, I gave my first philosophical lecture in this country. On that occasion I compared the new existentialist ideas, then spreading through Continental Europe, with the already classical pragmatist ideas predominant in this country. Since that time this country and the spirit of the two great universities—Columbia, including Union Theological Seminary, and Harvard—have purged my mind of many conscious and unconscious European provincialisms without, I hope, having replaced them with American versions of the same evil. A late fruit of this process of deprovincialization is my increasing interest, both as a theologian and as a philosopher of religion, in the encounters among the living religions of today and the encounter of all of them with the different types of secular quasi-religions. From this interest has arisen my present subject; the title of which indicates my intention to discuss the subject from the point of view of Christianity.

This intention requires both justification and interpretation. One can deal with such phenomena as the encounter of the world religions either as an outside observer who tries to draw the panorama of the present situation as factually as possible, or as a participant in the dynamics of the situation who selects facts according to his judgment of their relative importance, interprets these in the light of his own understanding, and evaluates them with reference to the *telos,* the inner aim he perceives in the movement of history generally, and in particular the history of religion. The latter procedure is followed here, but it should be noted that the two types of approach are not entirely independent of each other; they coalesce to a large degree. The outside observer is always an inside participant with a part of his being, for he also has confessed or concealed answers to the questions which underlie every form of religion. If he does not profess a religion proper, he nevertheless belongs to a quasi-religion, and as a consequence he also selects, judges, and evaluates. The theologian, on the other hand, who does this consciously from the ground of a particular religion, tries to grasp the facts as precisely as is humanly possible, and to show that there are elements in human nature which tend to become embodied in symbols similar to those of his own religion. This, in any case, is the way I, as an "observing participant," want to deal with the religious situation in a world-wide view.

I I

Where must we look if we want to draw a picture of the encounter of Christianity with the world religions? The answer to this question is by no means obvious, for the term religion is open both to limiting and to enlarging definitions, depending on the theological or philosophical position of him who defines. One can narrow the meaning of religion to the *cultus deorum* (the cult of the gods), thus excluding from the religious realm the pre-mythological as well as the postmythological stages, the first when there were not yet gods, and the second when there were no longer gods; e.g., shamanism at the one end of the development and Zen Buddhism at the other. Or one can include these two stages; then one must give a definition of religion in which the relation to gods is not a necessary element. And one can even take the further step of subsuming under religion those secular movements which show decisive characteristics of the religions proper, although they are at the same time profoundly different. It is in the latter, largest sense that I intend to use the term religion. This is required both by the Protestant background of my own philosophy of religion and by the present religious situation as I intend here to depict it.

The concept of religion which makes such a large extension of the meaning of the term possible is the following. Religion is the state of being grasped by an ultimate concern, a concern which qualifies all other concerns as preliminary and which itself contains the answer to the question of the meaning of our life. Therefore this concern is unconditionally serious and shows a willingness to sacrifice any finite concern which is in conflict with it. The predominant religious name for the content of such concern is God—a god or gods. In nontheistic religions divine qualities are ascribed to a sacred object or an all-pervading power or a highest principle such as the Brahma or the One. In secular quasi-religions the ultimate concern is directed towards objects like nation, science, a particular form or stage of society, or a highest ideal of humanity, which are then considered divine.

In the light of this definition I dare to make the seemingly paradoxical statement, that the main characteristic of the present encounter of the world religions is their encounter with the quasi-religions of our time. Even the mutual relations of the religions proper are decisively influenced by the encounter of each of them with secularism, and one or more of the quasi-religions which are based upon secularism.

Sometimes what I call quasi-religions are called pseudo-religions, but this is as imprecise as it is unfair. "Pseudo" indicates an intended but deceptive similarity; "quasi" indicates a genuine similarity, not intended, but based on points of identity, and this, certainly, is the situation in cases like Fascism and Communism, the most extreme examples of quasi-religions today. They are radicalizations and transformations of nationalism and socialism, respectively, both of which have a potential, though not always an actual religious character. In Fascism and Communism the national and social concerns are elevated to unlimited ultimacy. In themselves both the national and the social concerns are humanly great and worthy of a commitment even unto death, but neither is a matter of unconditional concern. For one may die for something which is conditional in being and meaning—as many Germans did who, for national reasons, fought under Hitler for Germany while hating National-Socialism and secretly hoping for its defeat. This conflict is avoided if the driving force in a national war is the defense of the vocational idea of the nation (p. 16). But even then it is not the nation as such, but the vocational idea (e.g., justice or freedom) which is a matter of ultimate concern. Nations and social orders as such are transitory and ambiguous in their mixture of creativity and destructiveness. If they are taken as ultimates in meaning and being, their finitude must be denied. This has been done, e.g., in Germany by the use of the old eschatological symbol of a "thousand-year period" for the future of Hitler's Reich, a symbol which originally signified the aim of all human history. The same thing has been done in Russia in terms of the Marxian type of eschatological thinking (classless society). In both cases it was necessary to deny the ambiguities of life and the distortions of existence within these systems, and to accept unambiguously and unconditionally their evil elements, e.g., by glorifying the suppression of individual criticism and by justifying and systematizing lie and wholesale murder—as happened in Italy and Germany and in Russia under Stalin. The quasi-religious character of any such "rule of an ideology" (or "ideocracy," as one might call it) makes these consequences unavoidable. But in such extremes something becomes manifest that, in a moderate way, characterizes all ideologically conscious movements and social groups. It is the consecration of communal self-affirmation, whether this consecration happens in religious or secular symbols. It is an element in every nationalism, whether among the old Asiatic or the new African nations, whether in Communist or in democratic countries. This quasi-religious element in all nationalism gives it its passion and strength, but also produces the radicalized nationalism which we denote here by a generalized term: Fascism. The same dialectics is true of Socialism. In it the expectation of a "new state of things" is the driving religious element, whether expressed in the Christian symbols of the end of history or in secular-utopian symbols like "classless society" as the aim of history. This quasireligious element in all Socialism was radicalized in the revolutionary period of Communism, and was, in its victorious period, reduced to an a-personal subjection under the demands of a neocollectivistic system. But even so the quasi-religious character persisted.

At this point I may be permitted to make a remark which is both personal and of objective importance. I refer to a movement in which an early encounter of religion and quasi-religion took place —the religious-socialist movement in the 1920s in Central Europe. It was an attempt to liberate the socialist ideology from absolutism, utopianism, and the destructive implications of a self-righteous rejection of criticism from beyond itself. It was the prophetic criticism, or the "Protestant Principle," which judges all religious or quasi-religious ab-

8

solutism, that we tried to introduce into the socialist self-interpretation—in vain for that time, completely in vain for Communist ideocracy, not quite
in vain for the socialist movements of present-day
Europe.

We have used nationalism with its Fascist radicalization, and socialism with its Communist
radicalization, as the most conspicuous examples
of quasi-religious movements in our time. One may
ask whether these are the only examples or whether
liberal humanism as dominant in most Western
countries can be understood as a quasi-religion of
equal power. This is not only a theoretical question,
but may well be the question of the capability of
the West to resist the onslaught of the quasi-religions in our present world. Liberal humanism and
its democratic expression are fragile forms of life,
rare in history, and easily undermined from within
and destroyed from without. In the periods of their
heroic fight against the absolutisms of the past,
their quasi-religious character was obvious, as was
their religious background. In the periods of their
victorious and mature development, their secular
character became predominant, but whenever they
had to defend themselves—as in matters of scien-

tific autonomy, educational freedom, social equality or civil rights—they showed again their quasi-religious force. It was a struggle between faith and faith; and the quasi-religious faith could be radicalized to a degree where it undercut even its own roots, as, for example, in a scientism which deprives all nonscientific creative functions, such as the arts and religion, of their autonomy. If in the foreseeable future a total defense of liberal humanism against Communism or Fascism should be necessary, a self-defying radicalization would take place and the loss of that very liberal humanism which is to be defended would be almost unavoidable.

At this point a significant analogy between liberal humanism and Protestantism becomes visible. Both Protestantism and early Christianity can be called religions of the Spirit, free from oppressive laws and, consequently, often without law altogether. But when they had to defend themselves, early Christianity against the Roman Empire and its quasi-religious self-deification, early Protestantism against the absolutism of the Church of the Counter Reformation, and modern Protestantism against that of the quasi-religious Nazi-Fascism, both had to surrender much of their Spirituality and to accept non-Christian and non-Protestant elements of legalism and authoritarianism. Religions of the Spirit, in the encounter with centralized and legally organized religions, are as fragile as the liberal-humanist quasi-religions; and there is a deep interrelation, in many cases interdependence, between the two. Therefore, with hesitation and anxiety I feel obliged to ask the question: Is historical mankind able to stand the freedom of a Spiritual religion and of a humanist quasi-religion for more than a short period? Unfortunately, the unanimous testimony of history is that it cannot. The real danger is not that they are overwhelmed by other less fragile forms of religion or quasi-religion, but that in defending themselves they are led to violate their very nature and shape themselves into the image of those who attack them. In such a critical moment we are living today.

Up to now we have answered the question, "Where to look if one wants to see the encounter of the world religions?", by introducing the concept and the types of quasi-religions which constitute the dynamic element in and above all other encounters. We kept the consideration of the two types of religion proper—the theistic and the nontheistic—in the background. They will now appear in the panorama we are painting, but more in their role as objects than as subjects in the historical encounter. (Their full description and evaluation is discussed in following chapters.)

III

The dramatic character of the present encounter of the world religions is produced by the attack of the quasi-religions on the religions proper, both theistic and nontheistic. The chief and always effective weapon for this attack is the invasion of all religious groups by technology with its various waves of technical revolution. Its effect was and is, first of all, a secularization which destroys the old traditions, both of culture and religion. This is most obvious in a country like Japan. The Christian missionaries there told me that they are much less worried about Buddhism and Shintoism than about the enormous amount of indifference towards all religions. And if we look at the religious situation as it prevailed in the second half of the nineteenth century in Europe, we find the same phenomenon. In a congregation of 100,000 people in East Berlin the main service often attracted no more than 100, mostly elderly women—no men, no youth. Christianity simply was not prepared for the technological invasion and its secularizing influences, nor are the religions in modern Japan. And the same must be said of the Greek Orthodox Church in Eastern Europe and of Confucianism, Taoism, and Buddhism in China. We must also add, though with qualifications, Indian Hinduism and the African tribal religions, and with rather strong qualifications, the Islamic nations. The first time Christian leaders officially observed the threat of this situation was at the conference of the International Missionary Council in Jerusalem in 1928, but it was decades before this awareness influenced the Christian churches' view of themselves in relation to the world religions and to the international secular consciousness of mankind. Today the problems which have arisen out of this situation can no longer be neglected.

The first effect of the technological invasion of the traditional cultures and religions is secularism and religious indifference. Indifference towards the question of the meaning of one's existence is a transitory stage, however; it cannot last, and it never lasted longer than the one moment in which a sacred tradition has lost its meaning and a new answer has not yet appeared. This moment is so short because in the depth of technical creativity, as well as in the structure of the secular mind, there are religious elements which have come to the fore when the traditional religions have lost their power. Such elements are the desire for liberation from authoritarian bondage, passion for justice, scientific honesty, striving for a more fully developed humanity, and hope in a progressive transformation of society in a positive direction. Out of these elements which point back to older traditions the new quasi-religious systems have arisen and given new answers to the question of the meaning of life.

Secularism in the sense of a technical civilization has paved the way, often only within small upper classes, for the quasi-religions which have followed and offered an alternative to the old traditions as well as to mere indifference.


IV

Let us first look at nationalism and its ways of invading cultural and religious traditions. Nationalism is ultimately rooted in the natural and necessary self-affirmation of every social group, analogous to that of every living being. This self-affirmation has nothing to do with selfishness (though it may be distorted into selfishness). It is the "love of oneself" in the sense of the words of Jesus about loving one's neighbor "as oneself." Such self-affirmation is, in presecular periods, consecrated and protected by sacramental rites and oaths; the group and its religion are indistinguishable. Nationalism in the modern sense of the word can appear only when secular criticisms have dissolved the identity of religious consecration and group self-affirmation, and the consecrating religion is pushed aside and the empty space filled by the national idea as a matter of ultimate concern. In the West this development continued after the Renaissance and the Enlightenment, symbolized in the names of Machiavelli and Hobbes and intensified by the rise of the secular state over the fighting Christian confessions and their destructive encounters.

A nation is determined by two elements, its natural self-affirmation as a living and growing power-structure, and, at the same time, the consciousness of having a vocation, namely, to represent and spread and defend a principle of ultimate significance. It is the unity of these two elements which makes the quasi-religious character of nationalism possible. The examples are abundant: the Hellenic people were conscious of representing culture as against the barbarians; Rome represented the law; the Jews the divine covenant with man; and medieval Germany the *corpus Christianum,* religiously and politically. The Italians were the nation of the rebirth (*Rinascimento*); the British represented a Christian humanism for all nations, especially the primitive ones; France represented the highest contemporary culture; and Russia the saving power of the East against the West; China was the land of the "center," which all lesser nations encircled. And America is the land of the new beginning and the defender of freedom. And now this national idea has reached almost all parts of the world and has shown both its creative and its destructive possibilities.

The basic problem is the tension between the power and the vocational elements in national life. There is no nation in which the power element is lacking, in the sense of power to exist as an organized group at a definite place at a definite time. Yet there are cases, though not very frequent, in which the vocational element is minimized by the power element. Examples are Bismarck's Germany and Tojo's Japan. Hitler felt this lack and invented the salvation-myth of the Nordic race. Present-day Japan is looking for a vocational symbol. The future of all Asiatic and African nationalisms is dependent upon the character of their vocational consciousness and its relation to their will to power. If their quasi-religious claim is only a claim to national power, it is demonic and self-destructive; if it is united with a powerful vocational consciousness, imperialism can develop with a good conscience and produce empires in which creative and destructive elements are mixed. If the national consciousness is humanized and becomes aware both of its own finite validity and the infinite significance of that which it represents (though ambiguously), a nation can become a representative of the supra-national unity of mankind—in religious language, of the Kingdom of God.

There are nations in which the religious-vocational element still controls the mere power element, but they all are threatened by an inner transformation under the attack of the protagonists of unrestricted power politics—even if this is done in the name of a vocation, as in present-day Russia.

v

The "invasion" of Russia by its own Communist intelligentsia was one of the great events in the encounter of the world religions. It produced the most powerful dynamics in the struggle of quasi-religions with many religions in the proper sense. The invasion of Russia by Communism can be compared with the invasion of Eastern Christianity by Islam. The similarity lies in the identity of the invaded group and the structural analogy between the Mohammedan religion and the Communist quasi-religion. Both have decisive roots in Old Testament prophetism as well as in late Jewish legalism. Both have attacked a static sacramental system which had failed to extend its Spirituality to social criticism, as well as to criticism of its own superstitious distortions. So it could not resist the earlier nor the present onslaughts of a tremendously dynamic type of ultimate concern in which a vision of the future was the decisive element. Of course, the difference is that the religious hope is transcendent and the quasi-religious hope immanent, but the difference is much smaller from the psychological than from the theological point of view. The identification with the collective, the disregard of one's individual existence, the utopian spirit—these are equal in both.

It is this spirit which has also conquered the social ethical system of Confucianism, as well as the sacramental and mystical religions of Taoism and Buddhism, in China. With respect to the two latter, the situation was similar to that of Russian Orthodoxy: a lack of prophetic criticism derived from the ultimate religious concern, and a lack of self-criticism with respect to their mechanization and superstitious deterioration. In Confucianism, Communism encountered a system which, in spite of its cosmic-religious background, had first of all a social and ethical character, but which had lost this power with the disintegration of the hierarchy of governing officials and, at the same time, of the great-family-type of social coherence.

If we look at the invasion of the Russian satellite countries in Eastern Europe, the situation is different; here it was, in many cases, Roman Catholicism

which the Communists encountered, a world organization subject to a radically centered authoritarian guidance. Yet in spite of its authoritarian
character, elements of ancient thought, modern
liberal humanism and religious socialism are present. The war brought external conquest to these
countries, but a spiritual victory was never won by
the Communist quasi-religion. The same is true of
the Protestant population in Eastern Germany,
which has today the most admirable Church in
Protestantism. (But one must not forget that Eastern Europe, although large parts of it missed the
Reformation and the Renaissance, was continu-
ously influenced by liberal-humanist infusions
from the West.)

I referred to the analogy between Islam and
Communism in their attacks on Eastern Christianity. This makes it immediately understandable
that Islam was and is capable of resisting Communism almost completely. The social and legal
organization of the whole of Islam, as well as of
the daily life of the individual, gives a feeling of
social and personal security which makes it impreg-
nable to the Communist ideology, at least for the
present. But I must add that it makes it impregna-

ble to Christianity also. Nevertheless, it is not closed to secularism in connection with science and technology, and it is wide open to the entrance of nationalism.

One further question with respect to the encounter of Communism with the religions of the world must be considered, namely its encounter with the religions which are not world religions—the primitive religions which are still the ground of the newly independent African nations. Here a battle takes place in defense of their sacramental traditions, preserved not only by medicinemen, elders, and other representatives, but also by the deep anxiety of the masses who experience the breakdown of their security-providing rites and beliefs through the invasion of secularism and, following that, the invasion of foreign religions and quasi-religions, fighting with each other over the souls and bodies of the natives. If we look at the moves and counter-moves in these struggles we may find the following general situation: The very fact of their recent liberation from colonial control works in favor of a quasi-religious valuation of the national idea, but there is a limit to this loyalty. Tribes are not nations, and the present independent states are based on colonial divisions without sufficient communal coherence within their political boundaries, and often with more coherence with territories beyond them. In spite of these limits the national idea is a strong barrier against the Communist quasi-religion, while, on the other hand, the poverty of the masses provides a temptation which pulls in the opposite direction. In this situation neither the chances of liberal humanism nor those of Christianity are very great, and amongst the world religions it is Islam which has the greatest impact on sub-Saharan Africa, as it had 1300 years ago on Mediterranean Africa. As the religion of a simplified law and a simplified myth without racial discrimination, it is a more adequate faith for people whose collectivistic past keeps them still far from the personal problems of sin and grace which are central in Christianity. As for the religions of Indian origin, it seems that their transmundane centeredness has no appeal for these people with their tremendous vitality even under the hardest conditions.

A riddle which will sooner or later assume world historical significance is India and the large area of Southeast Asia in which Indian, Malayan, and

Chinese influences are mixed. Here, first of all, Hinduism and Buddhism continue as the basic religious tradition. Secondly, there has been and still is the invasion of all these countries by Islam, an invasion which split India in two at the moment of her independence. In official India a limited nationalism with some influences from Christianity and liberal humanism is present in the upper classes, though the Hinduist traditions are by far the most predominant in all classes. But, as we shall see more fully later, neither Hinduism nor Buddhism gives decisive motives for social transformation, and this provides a nonpolitical opportunity for an invasion of Hinduist India and Buddhist East Asia by the Communist quasi-religion with its hope for a transformed world. The question is, however, whether India's mystical spirituality will resist such an invasion, passively or perhaps even actively.

The encounter of Communism with the West cannot be discussed here in terms of the political conflict and its possible military consequences, but we must discuss it from the point of view of the cultural and spiritual encounter. The situation is the following: Judaism, Christianity, and Islam are comparatively immune to the Communist impact because all of them, and particularly prophetic Judaism, are the ultimate source of the revolutionary movements of the West, out of which Communism finally developed. The three religions which originated in Israel still have, despite all their secularism, nationalism, and organized injustice, the prophetic quest for justice as their essence. They were the soil in which Communism grew, but they are also the most unreceptive to their own matured and badly corrupted product, as long as the quest for justice is alive in them.

In all the encounters discussed so far, the two forms of religion which I have characterized as fragile—Spiritual Protestant religion and liberal humanist quasi-religion—played a small role, except in their power of resistance to Communism and their lack of resistance to nationalism. There is an Asiatic country (of which I have a personal knowledge) in which the encounter of these two with the Shintoist-Buddhist reality has become significant—Japan. There is hardly another Asiatic country in which the invasion of a technological civilization and of a religiously indifferent secularism has made such progress. On the other hand, the liberal-humanist and the Christian-Protestant ideas are an important reality in Japan, not measurable by statistics. Japan has gratefully received democracy from the hands of its conqueror, but democracy needs spiritual roots as well as sociologically favorable conditions. And they are lacking. Neither Shintoism nor Buddhism—and most Japanese are adherents of both religions at the same time—has symbols or ideas which can become productive and protective for democracy. Thus it was possible for a demonically radicalized militaristic Fascism to come into power. It is now as hated in Japan as Nazism is in Germany, and the thinking people have asked themselves about the spiritual roots of democracy, and asked me to lecture on the subject. They are not afraid of a victory for Communism; the highly developed individualism of the peasants and the lower and higher middle classes of the cities make Communist neocollectivism abhorrent to them. Yet they know there is a vacuum in their culture today, and they ask consciously: What is to fill it? This question is the universal question of mankind today.

Two

## CHRISTIAN PRINCIPLES OF JUDGING NON-CHRISTIAN RELIGIONS

IN the discussion of our general subject, "Christianity and the Encounter of the World Religions," we gave in our first chapter a view of the present situation, a view which was centered in the encounter of the quasi-religions with the religions proper. We discussed the encounter of nationalism (and its Fascist radicalization), of socialism (and its Communist radicalization), of liberal humanism (and its precarious situation), with the primitive sacramental religions, with the mystical religions of Indian origin, and with the ethical religions born of Israel. And we asked the question of the future of all religions in the face of the victory of secularism all over the world. We presented a panorama within which we did not give an elevated place to Christianity, but we now intend to look at the panorama from the point of view of Christianity.

First I want to ask the question: what has Christianity, in the course of its history, thought about other religions in general and certain religions in particular? How did it meet them? To what degree will this determine the encounter of Christianity with the world religions today? And above all: what has been and what will be the attitude of Christianity to the powerful quasi-religions which are, in their modern form, something new for Christianity?

Before going into this problem empirically I want to introduce a rather general consideration concerning all religions and, even more generally, all social groups. If a group—like an individual—is convinced that it possesses a truth, it implicitly denies those claims to truth which conflict with that truth. I would call this the natural self-affirmation in the realm of knowledge; it is only another word for personal certainty. This is so natural and so inescapable that I have never found even a sceptic who did not affirm his scepticism while contradicting everybody who denied its validity. If even the sceptic claims the right to affirm his scepticism (if he makes a statement at all), and to contradict those who doubt it, why should the member of a religious group be deprived of his "civil right," so to speak, of affirming the fundamental assertion of his group and of contradicting those who deny this assertion? It is natural and unavoidable that Christians affirm the fundamental assertion of Christianity that Jesus is the Christ and reject what denies this assertion. What is permitted to the sceptic cannot be forbidden to the Christian—or, for that matter, to the adherent of any other religion.

Consequently the encounter of Christianity with other religions, as well as with quasi-religions, implies the rejection of their claims insofar as they contradict the Christian principle, implicitly or explicitly. But the problem is not the right of rejecting that which rejects us; rather it is the nature of this rejection. It can be the rejection of everything for which the opposite group stands; it can be a partial rejection together with a partial acceptance of assertions of the opposite group; or it can be a dialectical union of rejection and acceptance in the relation of the two groups. In the first case the rejected religion is considered false, so that no communication between the two contradictory positions is possible. The negation is complete and under certain circumstances deadly for the one or the other side. In the second case some assertions and actions of the one or the other side are considered false, others true. This is more tolerant than the attitude of total negation, and it is certainly an adequate response to a statement of facts or ideas some of which may be true, some false, but it is not possible to judge works of art or philosophy or the complex reality of religions in this way. The third way of rejecting other religions is a dialectical union of acceptance and rejection, with all the tensions, uncertainties, and changes which such dialectics implies. If we look at the history of Christianity as a whole, we can point to a decisive predominance of this latter response in the attitude of Christian thinking and acting towards the non-Christian religions. But it is almost impossible to discover a consistent line of thought about this problem. And even less consistent is the attitude of Christianity to the contemporary quasi-religions. This observation contradicts the popular assumption that Christianity had an exclusively negative attitude toward other faiths. Indeed, nothing is farther from the truth. In this assumption a confusion frequently takes place between the attitude of the Christian churches toward Christian heretics, especially in the late Middle Ages, and their attitude toward members of other religions. The demonic cruelty of the former is in contrast with the comparative mildness of the latter.

The indefiniteness of the attitude toward strange religions starts in the Old Testament. In the earlier prophets, the pagan gods are treated as powers inferior to the power of Jahweh, particularly in foreseeing and determining the future, in hearing prayers, and in executing justice, but they are regarded as competing realities. Of course, in the long run, their loss of power led to their loss of being; a god without ultimate power is a "nothing," as they were later called. Jahweh has superior power because he is the God of justice. Since Amos, prophecy threatened Israel, the nation of Jahweh, with destruction by Jahweh because of its injustice. The covenant between Jahweh and the nation does not give the nation a claim to Jahweh's championship; he will turn against them if they violate justice. The exclusive monotheism of the prophetic religion is not due to the absoluteness of one particular god as against others, but it is the universal validity of justice which produces the exclusive monotheism of the God of justice. This, of course, implies that justice is a principle which transcends every particular religion and makes the exclusiveness of any particular religion conditional. It is this principle of conditional exclusiveness which will guide our further inquiry into the attitude of Christianity to the world religions.

Jesus' words are the basic confirmation of this principle. In the grand scene of the ultimate judgment (Matt. 25; 31ff.), the Christ puts on his right the people from all nations who have acted with righteousness and with that agape—love which is the substance of every moral law. Elsewhere Jesus illustrates this principle by the story of the Good Samaritan, the representative of a rejected religion who practices love, while the representatives of the accepted religion pass by. And when the disciples complain about people who perform works similar to theirs, but outside their circle, he defends them against the disciples. Although the Fourth Gospel speaks more clearly than the others of the uniqueness of the Christ, it interprets him at the same time in the light of the most universal of all concepts used in this period, the

concept of the Logos, the universal principle of the
divine self-manifestation, thus freeing the interpretation of Jesus from a particularism through which
he would become the property of a particular religious group. Further, in the talk with the Samaritan woman, Jesus denies the significance of any
particular place of adoration and demands an
adoration "in Spirit and in Truth."

Paul is in a situation which is typical of all later
developments. He has to fight on two fronts—
against the legalism of Christianized Jews and
against the libertinism of Christianized pagans.
He has to defend the new principle revealed in the
appearance of the Christ. But, as always, defense
narrows down. So his first condemnations are ut-
tered against Christian distorters of his message;
anathemas are always directed against Christians,
not against other religions or their members. With
respect to other religions he makes the assertion,
unheard of for a Jew, that Jews and pagans are
equally under the bondage of sin and equally in
need of salvation—a salvation which comes not
from a new religion, the Christian, but from an
event in history which judges all religions, including Christianity.

In early Christianity the judgment of other religions was determined by the idea of the Logos. The Church Fathers emphasized the universal presence of the Logos, the Word, the principle of divine self-manifestation, in all religions and cultures. The Logos is present everywhere, like the seed on the land, and this presence is a preparation for the central appearance of the Logos in a historical person, the Christ. In the light of these ideas Augustine could say that the true religion had existed always and was called Christian only after the appearance of the Christ. Accordingly, his dealing with other religions was dialectical, as was that of his predecessors. They did not reject them unambiguously and, of course, they did not accept them unambiguously. But in their apologetic writings they acknowledged the preparatory character of these religions and tried to show how their inner dynamics drives them toward questions whose answer is given in the central event on which Christianity is based. They tried to show the convergent lines between the Christian message and the intrinsic quests of the pagan religions. In doing so they used not only the large body of literature in which the pagans had criticized their own religions (for example, the Greek philosophers), but also made free use of the positive creations from the soil of the pagan religions. On the level of theological thought they took into Christianity some of the highest conceptualizations of the Hellenistic and, more indirectly, of the classical Greek feeling toward life— terms like physis (natura), hypostasis (substance), ousia (power of being), prosopon (persona, not person in our sense), and above all logos (word and rational structure in the later Stoic sense). They were not afraid to call the God to whom they prayed as the Father of Jesus, the Christ, the unchangeable One.

All these are well-known facts, but it is important to see them in the new light of the present encounter of the world religions, for then they show that early Christianity did not consider itself as a radical-exclusive, but as the all-inclusive religion in the sense of the saying: "All that is true anywhere in the world belongs to us, the Christians." And it is significant that the famous words of Jesus, "You, therefore, must be perfect, as your heavenly Father is perfect," (which was always an exegetic riddle) would, according to recent research, be better translated, "You must be all-inclusive as your heavenly Father is all-inclusive."

Besides the reception of basic concepts from pagan metaphysical thought, which always means implicitly religious thought, early Christianity adopted moral principles from the Stoics, who represented both a philosophy and a way of life—a process which is already present in the Paulinian letters. The early Church shaped its ritual structure in analogy with that of the mystery religions, some of which were its serious competitors, and used the Roman legal and the Germanic feudal forms for its social and political self-realization, while on the more popular, but officially accepted, level it has, through the veneration of saints, appropriated and transformed many genuine pagan motifs and symbols.

II

This astonishing universalism, however, was always balanced by a criterion which was never questioned, either by the orthodox or by the heretical groups: the image of Jesus as the Christ, as documented in the New, and prepared for in the Old Testament. Christian universalism was not syncretistic; it did not mix, but rather subjected whatever it received to an ultimate criterion. In the power of this polarity between universality and concreteness it entered the Medieval period, having to compete with no religion equal to it in either of these respects. In both the Mediterranean and the northern half of Western civilization the one all-embracing religion and the one all-embracing culture were amalgamated into a unity of life and thought. All conflicts, however severe, occurred within this unity. No external encounters disturbed it.

But in the seventh century something happened which slowly changed the whole situation. The first outside encounter took place with the rise of Islam, a new and passionate faith, fanatically carried over the known world, invading, subjecting, and reducing Eastern Christianity and threatening all Christendom. Based on Old Testament, pagan, and Christian sources, and created by a prophetic personality, it was not only adapted to the needs of primitive tribes, but also capable of absorbing large elements of the ancient culture, and soon surpassed Western Christianity in culture and civilization. The shock produced by these events can be compared only with the shock produced by the establishment of the Communist quasi-religion in Eastern Europe, Russia, and China, threatening Western Christianity and its liberal-humanist quasi-religious transformation.

The victorious wars of the Islamic tribes and nations forced Christianity to become aware of itself as one religion confronted with another against which it had to defend itself. According to the law that defense narrows down the defender, Christianity became at this point radically exclusive. The Crusades were the expression of this new self-consciousness. They were the result of the first encounter of Christianity with a new world religion. (This analogy, to leap to the present for a moment, makes understandable the crusading spirit of this country against the two radicalized types of quasi-religions —Fascism on the one hand, Communism on the other. The often irrational and almost obsessive character of this crusading spirit shows that here expressions of ultimate concern are at work, though deeply ambiguous ones. Their ambiguity shows itself also in the fact that, just as in the period of the Crusades, they conflict with sober political judgment and profounder religious insight.)

The irrational character of the crusading spirit

was confirmed by the fact that the narrowed self-consciousness, created by the encounter of Christianity with Islam, produced also a changed self-consciousness with respect to the Jews. Since the period of the New Testament, and expressed most clearly in the Johannine literature, a Christian anti-Judaism has existed, based, of course, on the rejection of Jesus as the Messiah by the vast majority of the Jews. Nevertheless, they were tolerated and often welcomed in the earlier period; the Church waited for their conversion. But after the shock of the encounter with Islam the Church became conscious of Judaism as another religion and anti-Judaism became fanatical. Only after this was it possible for governments to use the Jews as political scapegoats to cover up their own political and economic failures, and only since the end of the nineteenth century did religious anti-Judaism become racial anti-Semitism, which was—and still is—one of the many ingredients in the radicalized nationalistic quasi-religion.

III

But the encounter of Christianity with a new

and an old world religion in the period of the Crusades worked not only for a fanatical exclusiveness; it also worked slowly in the direction of a tolerant relativism. In the same early thirteenth century in which Pope Innocent III gave the model for Hitler's Nürnberg laws against the Jews, there was created by Christian, Islamic, and Jewish forces the near-miracle of a tolerant humanism on the basis of current traditions at the court of Emperor Frederick II in Sicily. It took one to two centuries for similar ideas to come again to the surface, changing the Christian judgment of non-Christian religions in a radical way.

The great Cardinal and member of the Papal Court, Nicholas Cusanus, was able in the middle of the fifteenth century, in spite of his being an acknowledged pillar of the Roman Church, to write his book, *De Pace Fidei* (The Peace between the Different Forms of Faith). He tells how representatives of the great religions had a sacred conversation in heaven. The divine Logos explained their unity by saying: "There is only one religion, only one cult of all who are living according to the principles of Reason (the Logos-Reason), which underlies the different rites. . . . The cult of the gods everywhere witnesses to Divinity. . . . So in the heaven of (Logos-) Reason the concord of the religions was established."

The vision of Cusanus was an anticipation of later developments. Ideas appeared which renewed and even transcended the early Christian universalism, but without falling into relativism. People like Erasmus, the Christian humanist, or Zwingli, the Protestant Reformer, acknowledged the work of the Divine Spirit beyond the boundaries of the Christian Church. The Socinians, predecessors of the Unitarians and of much liberal Protestant theology, taught a universal revelation in all periods. The leaders of the Enlightenment, Locke, Hume, and Kant, measured Christianity by its reasonableness and judged all other religions by the same criterion. They wanted to remain Christians, but on a universalist, all-inclusive basis. These ideas inspired a large group of Protestant theologians in the nineteenth and early twentieth centuries. A symptom of this situation is the rise of philosophies of religion, the very term implying that Christianity has been subsumed under the universal concept of religion. This seems harmless enough, but it is not. In the periods in which the concrete element dominated and repressed the universalist element, the theologians were aware of this danger and they maintained a unique claim for Christianity by contrasting revelation—restricted to Christianity—with religion as designating every non-Christian religion. Or they called Christianity the true religion, all other religions "false religions." With the disappearance of this distinction, however, Christianity, while still claiming some superiority, stepped down from the throne of exclusiveness to which these theologians had raised it and became no more than the exemplar of the species religion. Thus Christian universalism was transformed into humanist relativism.

This situation is reflected in the way in which both philosophers and theologians, in their philosophies of religion, dealt with Christianity in relation to other religions. Kant, in his book on *Religion within the Limits of Pure Reason,* gives Christianity an exalted standing by interpreting its symbols in terms of his *Critique of Practical Reason.* Fichte uses the Fourth Gospel to exalt Christianity as a representative of mysticism; Schelling and Hegel consider it, in spite of Islam, as the fulfillment of all that is positive in the other religions and cultures; Schleiermacher gives a construction of the history of religions in which Christianity takes the highest place in the highest type of religion. My own teacher, Ernst Troeltsch, in his famous essay, "The Absoluteness of Christianity," asks most radically the question of the standing of Christianity among the world religions. He, like all the other Christian theologians and philosophers, who subsume Christianity under the concept of religion, construes Christianity as the most adequate realization of the potentialities implied in that concept. But since the concept of religion is itself derived from the Christian-humanist tradition, the procedure is circular. Troeltsch was aware of this situation and drew the consequences in his interpretation of history, in which he states no universal aim of history, but restricts himself to his own tradition, of which Christianity is an element. He calls it "Europeism"; today we would probably call it "The West." A consequence of this withdrawal was his advocation of the replacement of missionary attacks on the other world religions by "cross-fertilization," which was meant more as cultural exchange than as interreligious unity of acceptance and rejection. The resignation implied in this solution followed a general trend of nineteenth century thought, positivism in the original sense of the word, as acceptance of the empirically given without a superior criterion.

There was, however, always a majority of theologians and church people who interpreted Christianity in a particularistic and absolutistic way. They emphasized the exclusiveness of the salvation through Christ, following the main line of the theology of the Reformers, their orthodox systematizers and their pietistic transformers. In several waves the anti-universalist movements attacked the universalist trends which had become powerful in the last centuries. Every relativistic attitude towards the world religions was denounced as a negation of the absolute truth of Christianity. Out of this tradition (which is not necessarily fundamentalist in the ordinary sense) a strong particularistic turn of theology has grown. It was called in Europe crisis-theology; in America it is being called neo-orthodoxy. Its founder and outstanding representative is Karl Barth. This theology can be summed up from the point of view of our problem as the rejection of the concept of religion if applied to Christianity. According to him, the Christian

Church, the embodiment of Christianity, is based on the only revelation that has ever occurred, namely, that in Jesus Christ. All human religions are fascinating, but futile attempts of man to reach God, and the relation to them, therefore, is no problem; the Christian judgment of them is unambiguous rejection of their claim to be based on revelation. Consequently, the problem which is the subject of this book—the encounter of Christianity with the world religions—may be an interesting historical problem, but is not a theological one. Yet history itself forced the problem on Barth, not through an encounter with a non-Christian religion in the proper sense, but through a highly dramatic encounter with one of the radicalized and demoniacal quasi-religions—Nazism. Under Barth's leadership the European Christian churches were able to resist its onslaught; the radical self-affirmation of Christianity in his theology made any compromise with Nazism impossible. But, according to the law mentioned above, the price paid for this successful defense was a theological and ecclesiastical narrowness which blinded the majority of Protestant leaders in Europe to the new situation arising out of the encounters of religions and quasi-religions all over the world. The missionary question was treated in a way which contradicted not only Troeltsch's idea of a cross-fertilization of the high religions, but also early Christian universalism, and it deserves mention that Barth and his whole school gave up the classical doctrine of the Logos in which this universalism was most clearly expressed.

The present attitude of Christianity to the world religions is as indefinite as that in most of its history. The extreme contrast between men like Barth and the theologian of missions, Kraemer, on the one side, and Troeltsch and the philosophical historian, Toynbee, with his program of a synthesis of the world religions, on the other, is symbolic for the intrinsic dialectics of the relation of Christianity to the religions proper. Implications of this dialectics for the relation of Christianity to particular religions, especially those originating in India, will be discussed in a later chapter.

IV

We must still ask the question, at least in general terms, of what the attitude of Christianity to the quasi-religions is. The answer presupposes a discussion of the attitude of Christianity to the secular realm in general. I do not say to secularism, for there is no problem in this. Secularism, i.e., the affirmation of secular culture in contrast to, and to the exclusion of, religion can only be rejected by Christianity as well as by every other religion. But the secular realm does not necessarily affirm itself in the form of secularism; it can affirm itself as an element within an overarching religious system, as was the case in the Middle Ages. Under such conditions Christianity has used the creations of the secular realm, wherever found—in Egypt or Greece or Rome—for the building of its own life. In our own period Christianity has been able to accept the different technical and economic revolutions and, after some brief reactions, the scientific affirmations which underlie these transformations of our historical existence. The relation of Protestantism to the secular realm is the most positive, due to the Protestant principle that the sacred sphere is not nearer to the Ultimate than the secular sphere. It denies that either of them has a greater claim to grace than the other; both are infinitely distant from and infinitely near to the Divine. This stems from the fact that Protestantism was largely a lay movement, like the Renaissance, and that in its later development a synthesis between the Enlightenment and Protestantism was possible, while in Catholic countries, even today, Christianity and the Enlightenment are still struggling with each other. The danger of the Protestant idea, of course, is that the acceptance of secularism can lead to a slow elimination of the religious dimension altogether, even within the Protestant churches. The general attitude of the Christian churches to the secular realm determines their judgment about the quasi-religions which have arisen on the basis of secularism.

First of all, it is obvious that Protestantism is more open to and, consequently, a more easy prey of the quasi-religions. The Roman Church has denied to all three types of quasi-religion—the nationalist, the socialist, and the liberal-humanist—any *religious* significance. It did not reject the nationalist or socialist idea as such; the social ethics of the Catholic Church could deal positively with both ideas under the criterion of the church tradition. More complex, and on the whole negative, is the Catholic attitude to the liberal-humanist quasi-religion, for it is hardly possible to purge this movement of its religious implications. Totally opposed, however, is the Catholic Church to the quasi-religious radicalizations of nationalism and socialism, namely Fascism and Communism. The religious element of neither can be denied—even if this element is a dogmatic "atheism." This leads to the uncompromising rejection of Communism, and to the less passionate, but equally unambiguous, rejection of Fascism by the Catholic Church.

Its positive valuation of the secular makes the relation of Protestantism to the quasi-religions much more dialectical and even ambiguous. Protestantism can receive and transform the religious elements of the quasi-religions. It has done so in different ways with all three of them, but it has also partly—though never totally—succumbed to their radicalized forms. The Catholic Church has not been open to such reception of and subjection to the quasi-religions.

A few facts may show the ambiguous character of Protestantism in relation to the quasi-religions. The national idea was, since the reform councils of the fifteenth and the Reformation of the sixteenth centuries, a decisive tool in the fight of Christian groups against Rome. This was seen more clearly in England than anywhere else; Holland followed later, while in Germany Luther used national protests against Rome in defense of the Reformation without having a German nation behind him. Only in the late nineteenth century did the nationalism of the newly founded German Empire come into conflict with the Roman Church. When Nazism radicalized the nationalistic faith, certain Protestant groups succumbed to it, while the majority repulsed the demonic attack of the nationalistic quasi-religion. In the United States there is a kind of conservative Protestantism (religiously as well as politically) which supports, often fanatically, the nationalist quasi-religion. It is a symptom of the openness of Protestantism to the danger of what one could call nationalist apostasy.

Protestantism had, in its earlier stages, less affinity to movements for social justice than Catholicism. Its negative judgment about the human predicament made it conservative and authoritarian. Nevertheless, there were the spiritually strong (though politically weak) movements of Social Gospel and Christian Socialism, which tried to discuss and transform the religious element in the

50

Socialist faith and to use it for Protestant social ethics. Against the Communist radicalization and demonization of Socialism, the Protestant churches were as uncompromising as the Catholic church, but there is a strong desire in many Protestant groups not only to reject, but also to understand, what is going on in one-half of the inhabited world.

Protestantism has its most intimate relation with the liberal-humanist quasi-religion. In many cases, as in all forms of liberal Protestantism, a full amalgamation has taken place. In the first chapter I called both Protestantism and liberal humanism spiritual but fragile; in the last chapter we will deal more fully with their relation.

One thing should have become clear through the preceding descriptions and analyses: that Christianity is not based on a simple negation of the religions or quasi-religions it encounters. The relation is profoundly dialectical, and that is not a weakness, but the greatness of Christianity, especially in its self-critical, Protestant form.

Three


A  CHRISTIAN-BUDDHIST

CONVERSATION


In the first chapter we drew a panorama of the
present encounters of religions and quasi-religions
in many areas. We did it with a particular emphasis on the quasi-religions, their nature and their
superior historical dynamics. It was the encounter
of nationalism, communism and liberal humanism
with the religions proper which was at the center
of our interest, because it is decisive for our present
religious situation. In the second chapter Christian
principles of judging non-Christian religions were
discussed and the universalism of Christian theology in most centuries was shown. We illustrated
with examples from the history of the Church the
Christian belief that revelatory events underlie all
religions and quasi-religions, but also the theological idea that the revelatory event on which Chris-

tianity is based has critical and transforming power for all religions.

On the basis of this judgment of the non-Christian religions and quasi-religions on the part of Christianity, I intend now to discuss a concrete encounter of Christianity with one of the greatest, strangest, and at the same time most competitive of the religions proper—Buddhism. The discussion of this encounter will not be merely descriptive; it will be presented in a systematic way as a dialogue about the basic principles of both religions. In order to do this it is first necessary to determine the systematic place of both Christianity and Buddhism within the whole of man's religious existence. Such an attempt is perhaps the most difficult one in the comparative study of religions, but if successful it is the most fruitful for the understanding of the seemingly incomprehensible jungle which the history of religion presents to the investigating mind. It is the attempt to erect signposts pointing to *types* of religions, their general characteristics, and their positions in relation to each other.

The establishment of types, however, is always a dubious enterprise. Types are logical ideals for the sake of a discerning understanding; they do not exist in time and space, and in reality we find only a mixture of types in every particular example. But it is not this fact alone which makes typologies questionable. It is above all the spatial character of typological thinking; types stand beside each other and seem to have no interrelation. They seem to be static, leaving the dynamics to the individual things, and the individual things, movements, situations, persons (e.g., each of us) resist the attempt to be subordinated to a definite type. Yet types are not necessarily static; there are tensions in every type which drive it beyond itself. Dialectical thought has discovered this and has shown the immense fertility of the dialectical description of tensions in seemingly static structures. The kind of dialectics which, I believe, is most adequate to typological inquiries is the description of contrasting poles within one structure. A polar relation is a relation of interdependent elements, each of which is necessary for the other one and for the whole, although it is in tension with the opposite element. The tension drives both to conflicts and beyond the conflicts to possible unions of the polar elements. Described in this way, types lose their static rigidity, and the individual things and persons can transcend the type to which they belong without losing their definite character. Such a dynamic typology has, at the same time, a decisive advantage over a one-directed dialectics like that of the Hegelian school, in that it does not push into the past what is dialectically left behind. For example, in the problem of the relation of Christianity and Buddhism, Hegelian dialectics considers Buddhism as an early stage of the religious development which is now totally abandoned by history. It still exists, but the World-Spirit is no longer creatively in it. In contrast, a dynamic typology considers Buddhism as a living religion, in which special polar elements are predominant, and which therefore stands in polar tension to other religions in which other elements are predominant. In terms of this method, for example, it would be impossible to call Christianity the absolute religion, as Hegel did, for Christianity is characterized in each historical period by the predominance of different elements out of the whole of elements and polarities which constitute the religious realm.

However, one may point to the fact that we distinguish between living and dead religions on the one hand, and between high and low religions on the other hand, and ask: Does this not mean that some religions *did* disappear completely after the rise of higher forms, and could not Buddhism be considered, as it is with Hegel and in neo-orthodox theology, as a religion which is, in principle, dead? If this were so, a serious dialogue would be impossible. But it is not so! While specific religions, as well as specific cultures, do grow and die, the forces which brought them into being, the type-determining elements, belong to the nature of the holy and with it to the nature of man, and with it to the nature of the universe and the revelatory self-manifestation of the divine. Therefore the decisive point in a dialogue between two religions is not the historically determined, contingent *embodiment* of the typological elements, but these elements themselves. Under the method of dynamic typology every dialogue between religions is accompanied by a silent dialogue *within* the representatives of each of the participating religions. If the Christian theologian discusses with the Buddhist priest the relation of the mystical and the ethical elements in both religions and, for instance, defends the priority of the ethical over the mystical, he discusses at the same time within himself the relationship of the two in Christianity. This produces (as I can witness) both seriousness and anxiety.

It would now seem in order to give a dynamic typology of the religions or, more precisely, of the typical elements which, in many variations, are the determining factors in every concrete religion. But this is a task which by far transcends the scope of this book, which may be considered as a small contribution to such a typology. The only statement possible at this moment is the determination of the polarities of which Christianity and Buddhism occupy the opposite poles. Like all religions, both grow out of a sacramental basis, out of the experience of the holy as present here and now, in this thing, this person, this event. But no higher religion remained on this sacramental basis; they transcended it, while still preserving it, for as long as there is religion the sacramental basis cannot disappear. It can, however, be broken and transcended. This has happened in two directions, the mystical and the ethical, according to the two elements of the experience of the holy—the experience of the holy as being and the experience of the holy as what ought to be. There is no holiness and therefore no living religion without both elements, but the predominance of the mystical element in all India-born religions is obvious, as well as the predominance of the social-ethical element in those born of Israel. This gives to the dialogue a preliminary place within the encounters of the religions proper. At the same time it gives an example of the encounter and the conflict of the elements of the holy within every particular religion.

II

Buddhism and Christianity have encountered each other since early times, but not much of a dialogue resulted from the encounter. Neither of the two religions plays a role in the classical literature of the other. Buddhism made its first noticeable impact on Western thought in the philosophy of Schopenhauer, who with some justification identified his metaphysics and psychology of "will" with Indian, and especially Buddhist, insights. A second influx of Indian, including Buddhist, ideas occurred in the beginning of our century when Buddhist sources were published in attractive translations, and men like Rudolf Otto, the Marburg theologian and author of the classical book, *The*

*Idea of the Holy*, began a continuous and profound personal and literary dialogue between Christianity and the Indian religions. The discussion has been going on ever since both in the East and the West—in the East not only from the side of Indian Hinduism, but also from the side of Japanese Buddhism. This points to a third and more existential encounter, the missionary attack of Japanese Zen Buddhism on the Western educated classes, both Christian and humanist. (The reason for the success as well as the limits of this Buddhist invasion in the West will be discussed later.)

Is there a corresponding impact of Christianity on Buddhism? To answer this one must distinguish, as with respect to all Asiatic religions, three ways in which Christianity could have influenced them—the direct missionary way, the indirect cultural way, and the personal dialogical way. Missionary work has had a very slight impact on the educated classes of the Asiatic nations, although the conversion of outstanding individuals proves at least a qualitative success of the missions. But in a nation like Japan, where superior civilizing forces have shaped almost all classes of society, missionary success is very limited. In Indian Hinduism the masses are more open to Christian missionary work, as the South Indian church shows, but in the upper classes it is rather a Christian humanism which has taken hold of important individuals. For in all Asiatic religions the indirect, civilizing influence of Christianity is, for the time being, decisive, and not its missionary work. There is a third way, the dialogical-personal, of making inroads into Buddhist spirituality. It is immeasurable, quantitatively as well as qualitatively, but it is a continuous reality and the basis of the dialogical material to be given here.

If we look at the mutual influences between Christianity and Buddhism as a whole, we must conclude that they are extremely small—not comparable with the impact of Christianity on the Mediterranean and Germanic nations in the far past, and on many religiously primitive nations in the recent past, or with the impact Buddhism once had on the lower classes as well as the cultured groups of East Asia, for example in China and Japan. And, certainly, the mutual influence of the two religions cannot be compared with the tremendous influence the quasi-religions have had on both of them. So it may happen that the dialogue between them, in a not too distant future, will center on the common problems which arise with respect to the secularization of all mankind and the resulting attack of the powerful quasi-religions on all religions proper. But even so the interreligious dialogue must go on and should bear more fruits than it has up to now.

A dialogue between representatives of different religions has several presuppositions. It first presupposes that both partners acknowledge the value of the other's religious conviction (as based ultimately on a revelatory experience), so that they consider the dialogue worthwhile. Second, it presupposes that each of them is able to represent his own religious basis with conviction, so that the dialogue is a serious confrontation. Third, it presupposes a common ground which makes both dialogue and conflicts possible, and, fourth, the openness of both sides to criticisms directed against their own religious basis. If these presuppositions are realized—as I felt they were in my own dialogues with priestly and scholarly representatives of Buddhism in Japan—this way of encounter of two or more religions can be extremely fruitful and, if continuous, even of historical consequence.

One of the important points which is valid for all discussions between representatives of religions proper today is the unceasing reference to the quasi-religions and their secular background. In this way the dialogue loses the character of a discussion of dogmatic subtleties and becomes a common inquiry in the light of the world situation; and it may happen that the particular theological points become of secondary importance in view of the position of defense of all religions proper.

### III

The last remark leads immediately to the question to which all types of religions proper and of quasi-religions give an answer, whether they intend to do so or not. It is the question of the intrinsic aim of existence—in Greek, the *telos* of all existing things. It is *here* that one should start every inter-religious discussion, and not with a comparison of the contrasting concepts of God or man or history or salvation. They can all be understood in their particular character if the particular character of their concept of the telos has been understood. In the telos-formula of the Greek philosophers their whole vision of man and world was summed up, as when Plato called the telos of man ὁμοίωσις τῷ θεῷ κατὰ τὸ δυνατόν (becoming similar to the god as much as possible). In the dialogue between Christianity and Buddhism two telos-formulas can be used: in Christianity the telos of every*one* and everything united in the Kingdom of God; in Buddhism the telos of every*thing* and everyone fulfilled in the Nirvana. These, of course, are abbreviations for an almost infinite number of presuppositions and consequences; but just for this reason they are useful for the beginning as well as for the end of a dialogue.

Both terms are symbols, and it is the different approach to reality implied in them which creates the theoretical as well as practical contrast between the two religions. The Kingdom of God is a social, political, and personalistic symbol. The symbolic material is taken from the ruler of a realm who establishes a reign of justice and peace. In contrast to it Nirvana is an ontological symbol. Its material is taken from the experience of finitude, separation, blindness, suffering, and, in answer to all this, the image of the blessed oneness of everything, beyond finitude and error, in the ultimate Ground of Being.

In spite of this profound contrast a dialogue between the two is possible. Both are based on a negative valuation of existence: the Kingdom of God stands against the kingdoms of this world, namely, the demonic power-structures which rule in history and personal life; Nirvana stands against the world of seeming reality as the true reality from which the individual things come and to which they are destined to return. But from this common basis decisive differences arise. In Christianity the world is seen as creation and therefore as essentially good; the great Christian assertion, *esse qua esse bonum est,* is the conceptualization of the Genesis story in which God sees everything he has created "and behold, it was very good." The negative judgment, therefore, in Christianity is directed against the world in its existence, not in its essence, against the fallen, not the created, world. In Buddhism the fact that there is a world is the result of an ontological Fall into finitude.

The consequences of this basic difference are immense. The Ultimate in Christianity is symbolized in personal categories, the Ultimate in Buddhism in transpersonal categories, for example, "absolute non-being." Man in Christianity is responsible for the Fall and is considered a sinner; man in Buddhism is a finite creature bound to the wheel of life with self-affirmation, blindness, and suffering.

## IV

It seems that here the dialogue would come to an end with a clear statement of incompatibility. But the dialogue goes on and the question is asked whether the nature of the holy has not forced both sides to include, at least by implication, elements which are predominant in the other side. The symbol "Kingdom of God" appears in a religious development in which the holiness of the "ought to be" is predominant over the holiness of the "is," and the "protesting" element of the holy is predominant over the "sacramental" one. The symbol appears in prophetic Judaism, in the synoptic type of early Christianity, in Calvinism, and in the social type of liberal Protestantism. But if we look at Christianity as a whole, including the types just mentioned, we find a large amount of mystical and sacramental elements, and consequently ideas concerning God and man which approximate Buddhist concepts. The *esse ipsum*, being itself, of the classical Christian doctrine of God, is a transpersonal category and enables the Christian disputant to understand the meaning of absolute nothingness in Buddhist thought. The term points to the unconditional and infinite character of the Ultimate and the impossibility of identifying it with anything particular that exists. Vice versa, it is obvious that in Mahajana Buddhism the Buddha-Spirit appears in many manifestations of a personal character, making a nonmystical, often very primitive relation to a divine figure possible. Such observations confirm the assumption that none of the various elements which constitute the meaning of the holy are ever completely lacking in any genuine experience of the holy, and, therefore, in any religion. But this does not mean that a fusion of the Christian and the Buddhist idea of God is possible, nor does it mean that one can produce a common denominator by depriving the conflicting symbols of their concreteness. A living religion comes to life only if a new revelatory experience appears.

This dialogue leads to the general question of whether the controlling symbols, Kingdom of God and Nirvana, are mutually exclusive. According to our derivation of all religious types from elements in the experience of the holy, this is unthinkable, and there are indications in the history of both symbols that converging tendencies exist. If in Paul the Kingdom of God is identified with the expectation of God being all *in* all (or *for* all), if it is replaced by the symbol of Eternal Life, or described as the eternal intuition and fruition of God, this has a strong affinity to the praise of Nirvana as the state of transtemporal blessedness, for blessedness presupposes—at least in symbolic language—a subject which experiences blessedness. But here also a warning against mixture or reduction of the concrete character of both religions must be given.

The dialogue can now turn to some ethical consequences in which the differences are more conspicuous. In discussing them it becomes obvious that two different ontological principles lie behind the conflicting symbols, Kingdom of God and Nirvana, namely, "participation" and "identity." One participates, as an individual being, in the Kingdom of God. One is identical with everything that is in Nirvana. This leads immediately to a different relation of man to nature. The principle of participation can be reduced in its application to such a degree that it leads to the attitude of technical control of nature which dominates the Western world. Nature, in all its forms, is a tool for human purposes. Under the principle of identity the development of this possibility is largely prevented. The sympathetic identification with nature is powerfully expressed in the Buddhist-inspired art in China and Korea and Japan. An analogous attitude in Hinduism, dependent also on the principle of identity, is the treatment of the higher animals, the prohibition to kill them, and the belief, connected with the Karma doctrine, that human souls in the process of migration can be embodied in animals. This is far removed from the Old Testament story in which Adam is assigned the task of ruling over all other creatures.

Nevertheless, the attitudes towards nature in Christianity and Buddhism are not totally exclusive. In the long history of Christian nature-mysticism the principle of participation can reach a degree in which it is often difficult to distinguish it from the principle of identity, as, for example, in Francis of Assisi. Luther's sacramental thinking produced a kind of nature-mysticism which influenced Protestant mystics and, in a secularized form, the German romantic movement. It is not Christianity as a whole, but Calvinist Protestantism whose attitude towards nature contradicts almost completely the Buddhist attitude. In Buddhism the controlling attitude to nature increased with the migration of Buddhism from India through China to Japan, but it never conquered the principle of identity. Every Buddhist rock garden is a witness to its presence. The statement I heard, that these expressively arranged rocks are both here and, at the same time, everywhere in the universe in a kind of mystical omnipresence, and that their particular existence here and now is not significant, was for me a quite conspicuous expression of the principle of identity.

But most important for the Buddhist-determined cultures is the significance of the principle of identity for the relation of man to man and to society. One can say, in considerably condensed form, that participation leads to agape, identity to compassion. In the New Testament the Greek word agape is used in a new sense for that kind of love that God has for man, the higher for the lower, and that all men should have for one another, whether they are friends or enemies, accepted or rejected, liked or disliked. Agape in this sense accepts the unacceptable and tries to transform it. It will raise the beloved beyond himself, but the success of this attempt is not the condition of agape; it may become its consequence. Agape accepts and tries to transform in the direction of what is meant by the "Kingdom of God."

Compassion is a state in which he who does not suffer under his own conditions may suffer by identification with another who suffers. He neither accepts the other one in terms of "in spite of," nor does he try to transform him, but he suffers his suffering through identification. This can be a very active way of love, and it can bring more immediate benefit to him who is loved than can a moralistically distorted commandment to exercise agape. But something is lacking: the will to transform the other one, either directly, or indirectly by transforming the sociological and psychological structures by which he is conditioned. There are great expressions of compassion in Buddhist religion and art, as well as—and here again I can witness—in personal relations with friends, but this is not agape. It differs in that it lacks the double characteristic of agape—the acceptance of the unacceptable, or the movement from the highest to the lowest, and, at the same time, the will to transform individual as well as social structures.

Now the problem of history comes into the foreground of the dialogue. Under the predominance of the symbol of the Kingdom of God, history is not only the scene in which the destiny of individuals is decided, but it is a movement in which the new is created and which runs ahead to the absolutely new, symbolized as "the new heaven and the new earth." This vision of history, this really historical interpretation, has many implications of which I want to mention the following. With respect to the mode of the future, it means that the symbol of the Kingdom of God has a revolutionary character. Christianity, insofar as it works in line with this symbol, shows a revolutionary force directed towards a radical transformation of society. The conservative tendencies in the official churches have never been able to suppress this element in the symbol of the Kingdom of God, and most of the revolutionary movements in the West—liberalism, democracy, and socialism—are dependent on it, whether they know it or not. There is no analogy to this in Buddhism. Not transformation of reality but salvation from reality is the basic attitude. This need not lead to radical asceticism as in India; it can lead to an affirmation of the activities of daily life—as, for instance, in Zen Buddhism—but under the principle of ultimate detachment. In any case, no belief in the new in history, no impulse for transforming society, can be derived from the principle of Nirvana. If contemporary Buddhism shows an increased social interest, and if the sectarian "New Religions" in Japan (some of them of Buddhist origin) are extremely popular, this remains under the principle of compassion. No transformation of society as a whole, no aspiration for the radically new in history, can be observed in these movements. Again we must ask: Is this the end of the dialogue? And again I answer: Not necessarily. In spite of all the revolutionary dynamics in Christianity there is a strong, sometimes even predominant experience of the vertical line, for instance in Christian mysticism, in the sacramental conservatism of the Catholic churches, and in the religiously founded political conservatism of the Lutheran churches. In all these cases the revolutionary impetus of Christianity is repressed and the longing of all creatures for the "eternal rest in God, the Lord" approaches indifference towards history. In its relation to history Christianity includes more polar tensions than Buddhism, just because it has chosen the horizontal, historical line.

But this is not the end of the dialogue. For history itself has driven Buddhism to take history seriously, and this at a moment when in the Christian West a despair about history has taken hold of many people. Buddhist Japan wants democracy, and asks the question of its spiritual foundation. The leaders know that Buddhism is unable to furnish such a foundation, and they look for something which has appeared only in the context of Christianity, namely, the attitude toward every individual which sees in him a person, a being of infinite value and equal rights in view of the Ultimate. Christian conquerors forced democracy upon the Japanese; they accepted it, but then they asked: How can it work if the Christian estimation of every person has no roots either in Shintoism or in Buddhism?

The fact that it has no roots comes out in a dialogue like the following: The Buddhist priest asks the Christian philosopher, "Do you believe that every person has a substance of his own which gives him true individuality?" The Christian answers, "Certainly!" The Buddhist priest asks, "Do you believe that community between individuals is possible?" The Christian answers affirmatively. Then the Buddhist says, "Your two answers are incompatible; if every person has a substance, no community is possible." To which the Christian replies, "*Only* if each person has a substance of his own is community possible, for community presupposes separation. You, Buddhist friends, have identity, but not community." Then the observer asks: "Is a Japanese democracy possible under these principles? Can acceptance of a political system replace its spiritual foundation?" With these questions, which are valid for nations all over the non-Western world, the dialogue comes to a preliminary end.

Four


CHRISTIANITY JUDGING ITSELF

IN THE LIGHT OF ITS ENCOUNTER WITH

THE WORLD RELIGIONS


UNDER the general title, "Christianity and the Encounter of the World Religions," we gave first a view of the present situation, distinguishing between religions proper and secular quasi-religions. In drawing a map of their encounters all over the world we emphasized the fact that the most conspicuous encounters are those of the quasi-religions —Fascism, Communism, liberal humanism—with the primitive as well as the high religions, and that in consequence of this situation all religions have the common problem: how to encounter secularism and the quasi-religions based on it.

In the second chapter, under the title, "Christian Principles of Judging Non-Christian Religions," we tried to show a long line of Christian universalism affirming revelatory experiences in non-Christian religions, a line starting in the prophets and Jesus, carried on by the Church Fathers, interrupted for centuries by the rise of Islam and of Christian anti-Judaism, and taken up again in the Renaissance and the Enlightenment. This principle of universalism has been under continual attack by the opposite principle, that of particularity with the claim to exclusive validity, which has led to the unsettled and contradictory attitude of present-day Christianity towards the world religions. The same ambiguous attitude, we pointed out, is prevalent in the judgments of contemporary Christian leaders with respect to the quasi-religions and secularism generally.

In the third chapter, entitled "A Christian-Buddhist Conversation," we discussed, first, the problem of a typology of religions and suggested the use of a dynamic typology, based on polarities instead of antitheses, as a way of understanding the seemingly chaotic history of religions. As a most important example of such polarity Christianity and Buddhism were confronted, points of convergence and divergence shown, and the whole summed up in the two contrasting symbols, King-

dom of God and Nirvana. The chapter ended with
the question: How can a community of democratic
nations be created without the religions out of
which liberal democracy in the Western world
originally arose?

The last question leads us to the subject of this
chapter, "Christianity Judging Itself in the Light
of Its Encounters with the World Religions,"
meaning both religions proper and quasi-religions.

I

Let us consider first the basis of such self-judgment. Where does Christianity find its criteria?
There is only one point from which the criteria
can be derived and only one way to approach this
point. The point is the event on which Christianity
is based, and the way is the participation in the
continuing spiritual power of this event, which is
the appearance and reception of Jesus of Nazareth
as the Christ, a symbol which stands for the decisive self-manifestation in human history of the
source and aim of all being. This is the point from
which the criteria of judging Christianity in the
name of Christianity must be taken.

The way to this point is through participation, but how can one participate in an event of the past? Certainly not by historical knowledge, although we must listen to the witnesses to what happened; certainly not by acceptance of a tradition, although only through tradition can one be in living contact with the past; certainly not by subjecting oneself to authorities past or present, although there is no spiritual life without an actual (but not principal) dependence on authorities. Participation in an event of the past is only possible if one is grasped by the spiritual power of this event and through it is enabled to evaluate the witnesses, the traditions and the authorities in which the same spiritual power was and is effective.

It is possible, through participation, to discover in the appearance of the Christ in history the criteria by which Christianity must judge itself, but it is also possible to miss them. I am conscious of the fact that there is a risk involved, but where there is spirit, and not letter and law, there is always risk. This risk is unavoidable if one tries to judge Christianity in the name of its own foundation, but *if* it is done, it gives an answer to the question implied in the general subject of these lectures, "Christianity and the Encounter of the World Religions."

In the second chapter we discussed two tensions in the Christian self-interpretation, the first decisive for the relation of Christianity to the religions proper, and the second decisive for the relation of Christianity to the quasi-religions. The first is the tension between the particular and the universal character of the Christian claim; the second is the tension between Christianity as a religion and Christianity as the negation of religion. Both of these tensions follow from the nature of the event on which Christianity is based. The meaning of this event shows not in its providing a foundation for a new religion with a particular character (though this followed, unavoidably, with consequences partly creative and partly destructive, ambiguously mixed in church history), but it shows in the event itself, which preceded and judges these consequences. It is a personal life, the image of which, as it impressed itself on his followers, shows no break in his relation to God and no claim for himself in his particularity. What is particular in him is that he crucified the particular in himself for the sake of the universal. This liberates his image from bondage both to a particular religion

—the religion to which he belonged has thrown him out—and to the religious sphere as such; the principle of love in him embraces the cosmos, including both the religions and the secular spheres. With this image, particular yet free from particularity, religious yet free from religion, the criteria are given under which Christianity must judge itself and, by judging itself, judge also the other religions and the quasi-religions.

## II

On this basis Christianity has developed into a specific religion through a process of perpetuating the tradition of the Old Testament and, at the same time, of receiving elements from all the other confronted religions. As Harnack has said, Christianity in itself is a compendium of the history of religion. Although the first formative centuries were the most important in the whole development, the process has continued up to the present day. In it Christianity judged, was judged, and accepted judgment. The dynamic life it showed was nourished by the tension between judging the encountered religions in the strength of its founda-

tion, and accepting judgment from them in the
freedom its foundation gives. Christianity has in
its very nature an openness in all directions, and
for centuries this openness and receptivity was its
glory. But there were two factors which limited
more and more the freedom of Christianity to accept judgment: the hierarchical and the polemical.
With the strengthening of the hierarchical au-
thority it became increasingly difficult for it to
recant or to alter decisions made by bishops, councils and, finally, Popes. The tradition ceased to be
a living stream; it became an ever-augmented sum
of immovably valid statements and institutions.
But even more effective in this development was
the polemical factor. Every important decision in
the history of the church is the solution of a problem
raised by conflicts in history, and a decision, once
made, cuts off other possibilities. It closes doors,
it narrows down. It increases the proclivity to
judge, and it decreases the willingness to accept
judgment. The worst consequence of this tendency
was the split of the church in the period of the
Reformation and the Counter Reformation. After
that the glory of openness was lost to both sides.
The church of the Counter Reformation was in-

comparably less able to encounter the other religions or quasi-religions than the early church had been, and in the Protestant churches, in spite of the freedom the Protestant principle gives, it was only the influence of secularism which again opened them to a creative encounter with other religions. One sometimes points to the skill with which missionaries, especially in Catholic orders, adapt their message and their demands to the pagan substance of a superficially converted group. But adaptation is not reception and does not lead to self-judgment. In the light of this consideration we must acknowledge the degree to which Christianity has become a religion instead of remaining a center of crystallization for all positive religious elements after they have been subjected to the criteria implied in this center. Much of the criticism directed against Christianity is due to this failure.

With this general view in mind I want now to give examples of the way in which Christianity both judged other religions and accepted judgment from them, and finally to show the inner-Christian struggle against itself as a religion, and the new vistas which open up in consequence of these struggles for the future encounters of Christianity with the world religions.

Strictly in the Jewish tradition, the early Christians judged polytheism as idolatry, or the service of demonic powers. This judgment was accompanied by anxiety and horror. Polytheism was felt to be a direct attack on the divinity of the divine, an attempt to elevate finite realities, however great and beautiful, to ultimacy in being and meaning. The glory of the Greek gods impressed the Christians as little as did the animal-shaped divinities of the "barbaric" nations. But there arose a counter-judgment: the cultivated adherents of polytheistic symbolism accused the Jews and Christians of atheism, because they denied the divine presence in every realm of being. They were accused of profanizing the world. Somehow they were themselves aware of this fact. They did not moderate their abhorrence of polytheism, but they found many concrete manifestations of the divine in the world, for instance, hypostatized qualities or functions of God like His "Wisdom" or His "Word" or His "Glory." They saw in nature and history traces of angelic and demonic powers. Further—and in this Christianity parted ways with Judaism—they affirmed a divine mediator between God and man, and through him a host of saints and martyrs—mediators between the mediator and man, so to speak. In this respect Christianity has accepted influences from the polytheistic element of religion. In a secular form the conflict is alive even today as the conflict between a romantic philosophy of nature and its religious-artistic expressions, on the one hand, and the total profanization of nature and its moral and technical subjection to man's purposes, on the other.

I have chosen this example of a most radical judgment of another religious type by Christianity, which yet did not prevent the Christians from accepting judgment from it in turn.

Although it is itself based on the Old Testament, Christianity judged and still judges Judaism, but because of its dependence upon it, is most inhibited from accepting judgment from it. Nevertheless, Christians have done so since the removal of the barriers of medieval suppression which was born of anxiety and fanaticism. For almost two hundred years Christianity, by way of liberal humanism, has received Jewish judgment indirectly and has transformed the critique into self-judgment.

It was partly the resurgence of pagan elements in the national and territorial churches, and partly the suppression of the self-critical spirit in all churches, which called forth a prophetic reaction in democratic and socialist Christians.

I would like to be able to say more about judgment and the acceptance of judgment in relation to Islam, but there is little to say. The early encounter resulted only in mutual rejection. Are there possibilities for Christian self-judgment in these encounters? There are at two points—in the solution of the racial problem in Islam and in its wisdom in dealing with the primitive peoples. But this is probably all.

Another example of a radical rejection in connection with elements of acceptance was the dualistic religion of Persia, introduced into Christianity by Gnostic groups and supported by the Greek doctrine of matter resisting the spirit. The fight against dualism and the rejection of a God of darkness with creative powers of his own were consequences of the Old Testament doctrine of creation. For this Christianity fought, but the Christians were, at the same time, impressed by the seriousness with which dualism took the problem of evil; Augustine was for this reason a Manichean for ten years. There are also many Christians today who, with Augustine and his Protestant followers up to Karl Barth, accept the "total depravity" of man, a dualistic concept which was judged and accepted at the same time, and is being judged and accepted in present discussions for and against the existentialist view of man's predicament.

Christianity had encountered mysticism long before the modern opening up of India. A decisive struggle was made against Julian the Apostate's ideas of a restitution of paganism with the help of Neoplatonic mysticism. When we look at this struggle we find, on both sides, arguments similar to those used in our contemporary encounters with Indian mysticism. The Christian theologians were and are right in criticizing the nonpersonal, nonsocial and nonhistorical attitude of the mystical religions, but they had to accept the countercriticism of the mystical groups that their own personalism is primitive and needs interpretation in transpersonal terms. This has been at least partly accepted by Christian theologians who, in agreement with the long line of Christian mystics, have asserted that without a mystical element—namely, an experience of the immediate presence of the divine—there is no religion at all.

The examples could be multiplied, but these may suffice to illustrate the rhythm of criticism, countercriticism and self-criticism throughout the history of Christianity. They show that Christianity is not imprisoned in itself and that in all its radical judgments about other religions some degree of acceptance of counterjudgments took place.

### III

We have discussed the judgment of Christianity against itself on the basis of the judgment it received from outside. But receiving external criticism means transforming it into self-criticism. If Christianity rejects the idea that it is a religion, it must fight in itself everything by which it becomes a religion. With some justification one can say that the two essential expressions of religion in the narrower sense are myth and cult. If Christianity fights against itself as a religion it must fight against myth and cult, and this it has done. It did so in the Bible, which, one should not forget, is not only a religious but also an antireligious book.

The Bible fights for God against religion. This fight is rather strong in the Old Testament, where it is most powerful in the attack of the prophets against the cult and the polytheistic implications of the popular religion. In harsh criticism the whole Israelitic cult is rejected by some early prophets, and so is the mythology which gives the national gods ultimate validity. The God of Israel has been "demythologized" into the God of the universe, and the gods of the nations are "nothings." The God of Israel rejects even Israel in the moment when she claims Him as a national god. God denies His being *a* god.

The same fight against cult and myth is evident in the New Testament. The early records of the New Testament are full of stories in which Jesus violates ritual laws in order to exercise love, and in Paul the whole ritual law is dispossessed by the appearance of the Christ. John adds demythologization to deritualization: the eternal life is here and now, the divine judgment is identical with the acceptance or rejection of the light which shines for everybody. The early church tried to demythologize the idea of God and the meaning of the Christ by concepts taken from the Platonic-Stoic tradition.

In all periods theologians tried hard to show the transcendence of the divine over the finite symbols expressing him. The idea of "God above God" (the phrase I used in *The Courage To Be*) can be found implicitly in all patristic theology. Their encounter with pagan polytheism, i.e., with gods on a finite basis, made the Church Fathers extremely sensitive to any concept which would present God as being analogous to the gods of those against whom they were fighting. Today this particular encounter, namely with polytheism, no longer has manifest reality; therefore the theologians have become careless in safeguarding their idea of a personal God from slipping into "henotheistic" mythology (the belief in *one* god who, however, remains particular and bound to a particular group).

The early theologians were supported by the mystical element which in the fifth century became a powerful force in Christianity. The main concept of mysticism is immediacy: immediate participation in the divine Ground by elevation into unity with it, transcending all finite realities and all finite symbols of the divine, leaving the sacramental activities far below and sinking cult and myth into the experienced abyss of the Ultimate. Like the prophetical and the theological critique, this is an attack against religion for the sake of religion.

The ritual element was devaluated by the Reformation, in the theology of both the great reformers and of the evangelical radicals. One of the most cutting attacks of Luther was directed against the *vita religiosa*, the life of the *homini religiosi*, the monks. God is present in the secular realm; in this view Renaissance and Reformation agree. It was an important victory in the fight of God against religion.

The Enlightenment brought a radical elimination of myth and cult. What was left was a philosophical concept of God as the bearer of the moral imperative. Prayer was described by Kant as something of which a reasonable man is ashamed if surprised in it. Cult and myth disappear in the philosophy of the eighteenth century, and the Church is redefined by Kant as a society with moral purposes.

All this is an expression of the religious or quasi-religious fight against religion. But the forces which were fighting to preserve Christianity as a religion were ultimately stronger, in defense and counterattack. The main argument used in the counterattacks is the observation that the loss of cult and myth is the loss of the revelatory experience on which every religion is based. Such experience needs self-expression to continue, and that means it needs mythical and ritual elements. Actually they are never lacking. They are present in every religion and quasi-religion, even in their most secularized forms. An existential protest against myth and cult is possible only in the power of myth and cult. All attacks against them have a religious background, which they try to conceal, but without success. We know today what a secular myth is. We know what a secular cult is. The totalitarian movements have provided us with both. Their great strength was that they transformed ordinary concepts, events, and persons into myths, and ordinary performances into rituals; therefore they had to be fought with other myths and rituals— religious and secular. You cannot escape them, however you demythologize and deritualize. They always return and you must always judge them again. In the fight of God against religion the fighter for God is in the paradoxical situation that he has to use religion in order to fight religion.

It is a testimony to present-day Christianity that it is aware of this situation. We have mentioned the opposition to the concept of religion in the philosophy of religion as one of the symptoms of this fight. We have used the word demythologize. We have used the term quasi-religion to indicate that man's ultimate concern can express itself in secular terms. We find contemporary theologians (like Bonhöffer martyred by the Nazis) maintaining that Christianity must become secular, and that God is present in what we do as citizens, as creative artists, as friends, as lovers of nature, as workers in a profession, so that it may have eternal meaning. Christianity for these men has become an expression of the ultimate meaning in the actions of our daily life. And this is what it should be.

And now we have to ask: What is the consequence of this judgment of Christianity of itself for its dealing with the world religions? We have seen, first of all, that it is a mutual judging which opens the way for a fair valuation of the encountered religions and quasi-religions.

Such an attitude prevents contemporary Christianity from attempting to "convert" in the traditional and depreciated sense of this word. Many Christians feel that it is a questionable thing, for instance, to try to convert Jews. They have lived and spoken with their Jewish friends for decades. They have not converted them, but they have created a community of conversation which has changed both sides of the dialogue. Some day this ought to happen also with people of Islamic faith. Most attempts to convert them have failed, but we may try to reach them on the basis of their growing insecurity in face of the secular world, and they may come to self-criticism in analogy to our own self-criticism.

Finally, in relation to Hinduism, Buddhism, and Taoism, we should continue the dialogue which has already started and of which I tried to give an example in the third chapter. Not conversion, but dialogue. It would be a tremendous step forward if Christianity were to accept this! It would mean that Christianity would judge itself when it judges the others in the present encounter of the world religions.

But it would do even more. It would give a new valuation to secularism. The attack of secularism on all present-day religions would not appear as something merely negative. If Christianity denies itself as a religion, the secular development could be understood in a new sense, namely as the indirect way which historical destiny takes to unite mankind religiously, and this would mean, if we include the quasi-religions, also politically. When we look at the formerly pagan, now Communist, peoples, we may venture the idea that the secularization of the main groups of present-day mankind may be the way to their religious transformation.

This leads to the last and most universal problem of our subject: Does our analysis demand either a mixture of religions or the victory of one religion, or the end of the religious age altogether? We answer: None of these alternatives! A mixture of religions destroys in each of them the concreteness which gives it its dynamic power. The victory of *one* religion would impose a particular religious answer on all other particular answers. The end of the religious age—one has already spoken of the end of the Christian or the Protestant age—is an impossible concept. The religious principle cannot come to an end. For the question of the ultimate meaning of life cannot be silenced as long as men are men. Religion cannot come to an end, and a particular religion will be lasting to the degree in which it negates itself as a religion. Thus Christianity will be a bearer of the religious answer as long as it breaks through its own particularity.

The way to achieve this is not to relinquish one's religious tradition for the sake of a universal concept which would be nothing but a concept. The way is to penetrate into the depth of one's own religion, in devotion, thought and action. In the depth of every living religion there is a point at which the religion itself loses its importance, and that to which it points breaks through its particularity, elevating it to spiritual freedom and with it to a vision of the spiritual presence in other expressions of the ultimate meaning of man's existence.

This is what Christianity must see in the present encounter of the world religions.

p. 30, 31